I Love Ponie

Contents

Horses and Ponies

People began to tame, use and ride wild horses about 3,500 years ago. There are many different kinds, living all over the world. Some work and are useful. Some are kept for fun.

The story of the horse started in America more than **50** million years ago. Long before Man, there lived an animal called **Eohippus**. Over millions of years it changed and grew, and slowly started to look like a horse.

There are three main types of horse:
- **light horses**
- **heavy horses**
- **ponies**

Zebras, donkeys, asses and mules are members of the horse family.

Horses and ponies are measured in a unit called a **hand,** which is just over 10 centimetres. They are measured from the ground up to the **withers,** at the top of the shoulders.

Eohippus was much smaller than today's horse.

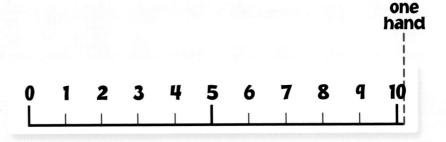

one hand

0 1 2 3 4 5 6 7 8 9 10

This is one hand. It measures **10.2** cm (**4** inches).
A **pony** is any horse that measures under **14.2** hands
(**145** cm/**57** inches).

A female pony is called a **mare.**
A male is called a **stallion.**
Babies are called **foals.**
Between 1 and 4 years old, male ponies are called
colts and female ponies are **fillies.**

There are more than 200 **breeds** or kinds of horse and pony.

Little

The Falabella is about **75** cm (**29** inches) tall.
The Shetland is about **85-100** cm (**33-39** inches).

and

Large

The largest heavy horse is the Shire. It is between **16** and **18** hands, and weighs about **1** tonne.

The parts of a pony's body are called the **points.** Some have special names.

croup

back

withers

neck

mane

ear

dock

eye

flank

muzzle

thigh

chest

knee

tail

fetlock

elbow

hoof

hock

Pony Breeds

Ponies can be different sizes and colours. Kinds of ponies that look the same are called breeds.

Riding ponies or crossbreeds are a mixture or cross of breeds. They can be any colour and up to **14.2** hands. They are the kind of pony many young riders ride.

breed name	colours	height (hh=hands)
Shetland	any colour, with long mane and tail	up to **42** inches (**107**cm)
Welsh	any solid colour, often grey	up to **13.2**hh
Exmoor	bay, brown or dun	**11.2–12.2**hh
Dales	mainly black or brown	**13.2–14.2**hh
Haflinger	palomino, chestnut with blond mane and tail	**13–14.2**hh
Connemara	mainly grey	**13–14.2**hh

Coats and colours
Most ponies are shades of brown or grey.

A white pony is always called a grey!

Ponies are covered in a **coat** of hairs. A pony's coat grows longer and thicker in cold weather, to keep it warm. In hot weather, it uses its long tail to swish away flies.

Coat colours have special names:

dun

bay

chestnut

dapple grey

palomino

skewbald

Most ponies have white **face markings**:

a **blaze** is a wide band down the face

a **stripe** is a narrow band

a **star** is a mark on the forehead

a **snip** is a mark on the muzzle

Some ponies have white **leg markings**:

a **stocking** is a white mark from the foot to the knee

a **sock** is a shorter white mark

a **coronet** is the white hair just above the hoof

7

Pony Talk

Ponies use body language and facial expressions to 'talk' to each other.
We can learn to understand what they are thinking and feeling.

Making Friends

To say 'hello' to a pony:

- Walk from the front at an angle, not from behind.
- Stand where it can see you, and say its name quietly.
- Stroke the neck gently. If a pony feels scared, it will run away.

Never shout, rush around or make sudden movements.
Be kind and gentle, and it will learn to trust you.

Smell

Ponies have a good sense of smell.

- Curl your fingers into your palm, hold out the back of your hand, and let the pony sniff it. The pony will get to know your scent.

Ponies love treats. Cut a carrot lengthways, not in rings or chunks, and place it flat on the palm of your hand.

Pony 'Talk'

How a pony looks and moves gives you clues about how it is feeling.

A pony's **ears** move all the time, listening to sounds all around. A pony's **ears** tell you a lot!

Ears relaxed, not forward or back, mean a pony is **happy**.

Ears laid back mean a pony is **uninterested**.

Ears laid flat back, nostrils flared and mouth open mean a pony is **cross**.

Ears back, eyes showing whites mean a pony is **frightened**.

Both ears pointing forward mean a pony is **alert** and **interested**.

Signs and Signals

When a pony rests a hind (back) leg it may be **tired**.

If a pony scrapes the ground with its hoof, it is **impatient**.

An **excited** pony will prance around with its tail held high.

An unusual smell or taste may make a pony curl its lip back. This is called **flehmen**.

9

Herd Life and Pony Paces

Wild ponies live in a large group called a herd. Ponies have good eyesight, sense of smell and hearing. They run fast to escape from danger or enemies.

Herds

Tame ponies kept in a field also like living with others. They are unhappy kept alone. An older pony will usually be in charge. It may nip and kick to show the others that it is the boss.

Touch is important. Two ponies may stand head to tail, nuzzling or nibbling each other's manes and backs. It shows that they are good friends! Ponies love to roll on their backs. It helps to remove loose hairs and dirt.

Mares and Foals

Mares (female ponies) have their babies in spring. They usually have one **foal**, but can have twins. A foal can walk very soon after being born. It drinks its mother's milk, then begins to graze on grass.

Teeth

Ponies eat grasses, which they crop with their sharp front teeth. People can tell the age of a pony by the number and size of its teeth, and whether they are worn down.

Speed

Racehorses can gallop at speeds of about **43** miles per hour (**70** kilometres per hour). Ponies are slower, but still speedy!

A pony's **pace** or **gait** is the way it moves. Humans have two gaits – walking and running – but ponies have four! Using different gaits, a pony can go faster or slower.

walk

The **walk** is the slowest pace, an even one-two-three-four. The pony always has at least two feet on the ground.

trot

The **trot** is a springy pace, with a moment when all four feet are off the ground.

canter

In the **canter** there are three beats, one-two-three, then a moment when all four feet are off the ground.

gallop

The **gallop** is the fastest pace, like a canter but faster, with a pony taking longer strides.

Clothes and Tack

Ponies wear special equipment called tack. Riders wear special clothes to keep them comfortable and safe.

A **riding hat** protects your head. It must fit well, with straps under the chin.

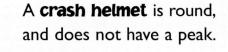

A **hard hat** is covered in velvet, with a peak. It can be covered by a coloured silk.

A **crash helmet** is round, and does not have a peak.

A loose **top** or **shirt** lets you move easily.

Gloves help you grip the reins.
  Thick ones keep hands warm in cold weather.
  Thin ones stop hands getting sweaty in hot weather.

A quilted **body warmer** keeps you warm and dry.

Jodhpurs are made of stretchy fabric. Special patches help you grip, and stop legs rubbing the saddle.

Strong **riding boots** protect *your* feet from pony feet!

Long **riding boots** fit closely and go almost to the knee.

Short **jodhpur boots** have a low heel.

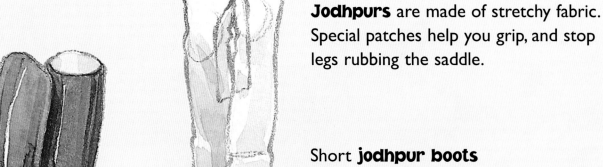

Tack is the equipment a pony wears. The main pieces are the **saddle** and **bridle**. Putting tack on is called **tacking up**. Taking it off is called **untacking**.

The **saddle** sits you on a pony's back. The main parts have special names:

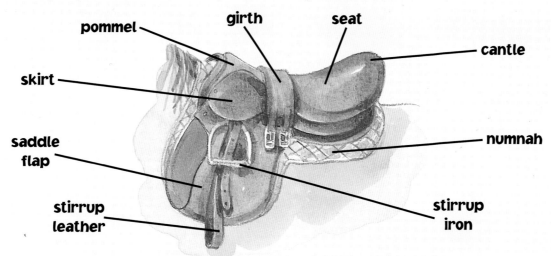

The **girth** fits around the belly to keep everything in place.

The **bridle** is a set of straps that fasten around a pony's head and hold a **bit** in its mouth. **Reins** attach to the bit. You move these to tell the pony what to do. The main parts of the bridle have special names:

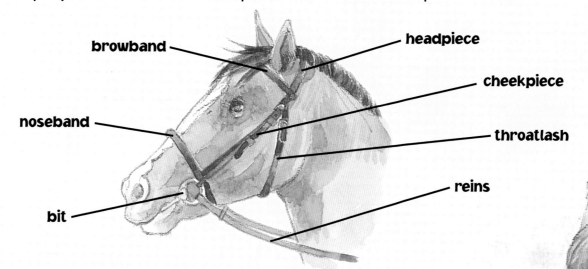

Rugs and **blankets** keep ponies warm and dry. Straps keep them in place even if a pony lies down or rolls.

A pony's **hooves** are like toenails. They need trimming every few weeks. Some ponies wear metal **horseshoes**. They are heated up, then nailed on. This does not hurt the pony!

   A person who looks after a pony's hooves is called a **farrier**.

13

Pony Care

Looking after ponies is hard work, and takes lots of time, but it's also great fun!

Some ponies live outside, in fenced **fields** or **paddocks**. They need:

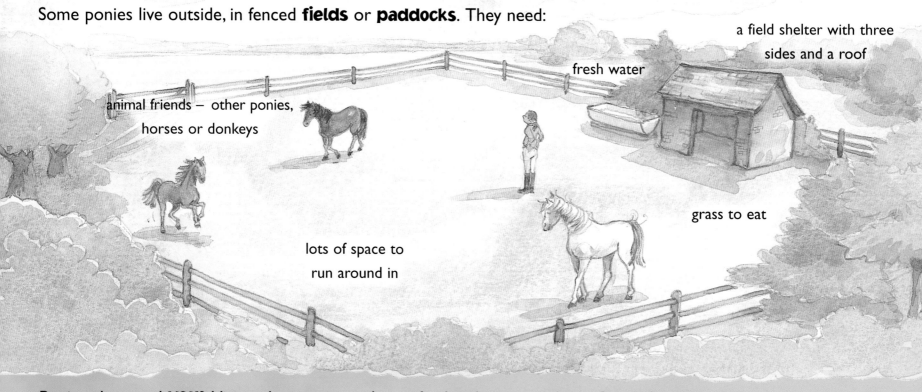

a field shelter with three sides and a roof

fresh water

animal friends – other ponies, horses or donkeys

grass to eat

lots of space to run around in

Ponies also need **YOU!** Visit at least twice a day, to feed and exercise them. Check for signs that a pony is not well:

- droopy head
- flat, still ears
- dull coat and eyes
- not eating

Vets care for sick ponies. **Horse dentists** look after horses' teeth.

Ponies that live outdoors, **at grass**, need the natural grease in their coats to keep them warm and dry. They should not be **groomed** too much.

They groom themselves by rolling, or rubbing against fences. They groom each other using lips and teeth.

! Some plants are **poisonous** and will make ponies **ill**. You must remove plants like:

! privet   **!** bracken   **!** acorns   **!** yew   **!** ragwort

Some ponies live indoors, in **stables**. A pony's 'room' is called a **loose box** or **stall**.

The floor has a thick covering of soft **bedding** so the pony can lie down without hurting itself. Making a pony's bed is called **bedding down**.

Bedding can be:
- straw
- shredded paper
- wood shavings

Mucking out means keeping the stable clean. Droppings and wet bedding must be removed and clean bedding added.

A **grooming kit** is used to look after a pony's coat and hair:

plastic or rubber curry combs
to take off dried mud

soft body brush to clean
the whole pony

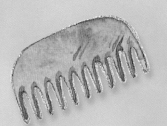

mane comb for
mane and tail

damp sponges to clean
eyes, nose and under tail

hoof pick to remove
stones from hooves

stable rubber to
polish the coat

Grass is a pony's main food. When there is not enough grass, ponies eat **hay**, which is dried grass. **Haynets** keep it off the floor.

Ponies eat other foods for extra energy, like:

✔ **pony nuts**　　✔ **bran**　　✔ **oats**　　✔ **barley**　　✔ **pieces of apple, carrot**

Riding School

Some people have a pony of their own. Others ride ponies that live in riding schools and stables.

A **riding school** is where you can learn about ponies and riding.
The **staff** know all about ponies and will teach you how to ride.

First Lessons

First lessons are in a **school**. Your teacher stands in the middle and tells you what to do. She may hold the pony on a long line called a **lunge rein**.

Your teacher or **instructor** will choose a quiet, kind pony that is the right size for you. You will learn how to **mount** (get on) and **dismount** (get off). You will learn to **sit up tall** in the saddle, and how to **hold the reins**.

Doing exercises like these before lessons will help you feel confident.

leaning back

swinging arms

Aids

You will learn about **'aids'**. These are the signals you give a pony to tell it what you want it to do. Aids are your **hands**, **legs** and **voice**. A trained pony knows what they mean.

Use aids to ask your pony to move forward, stop and turn, and to slow down or speed up. To go from halt (stop) to walk, press your lower legs into a pony's sides and say, **"Walk on."** Say, **"Good pony!"** when it does just that!

When you can ride, you can have all kinds of fun! **Hacking** is riding in the open. You must learn to do this safely, and use hand signals on roads.

Join a pony club and take part in **gymkhanas**, where riders and ponies race and play games.

In a **bending race** you steer your pony in and out of a row of poles.

In a **water race** you carry water to a bucket to see who can collect most.

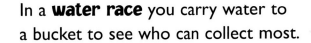

You can learn to **jump** poles and fences.
In **dressage tests**, a pony is given marks for doing special movements.

Well Done!
1st, **2nd** or **3rd** ponies in a test or competition win a rosette.
Even if it does not win, pat your pony as a reward for trying!

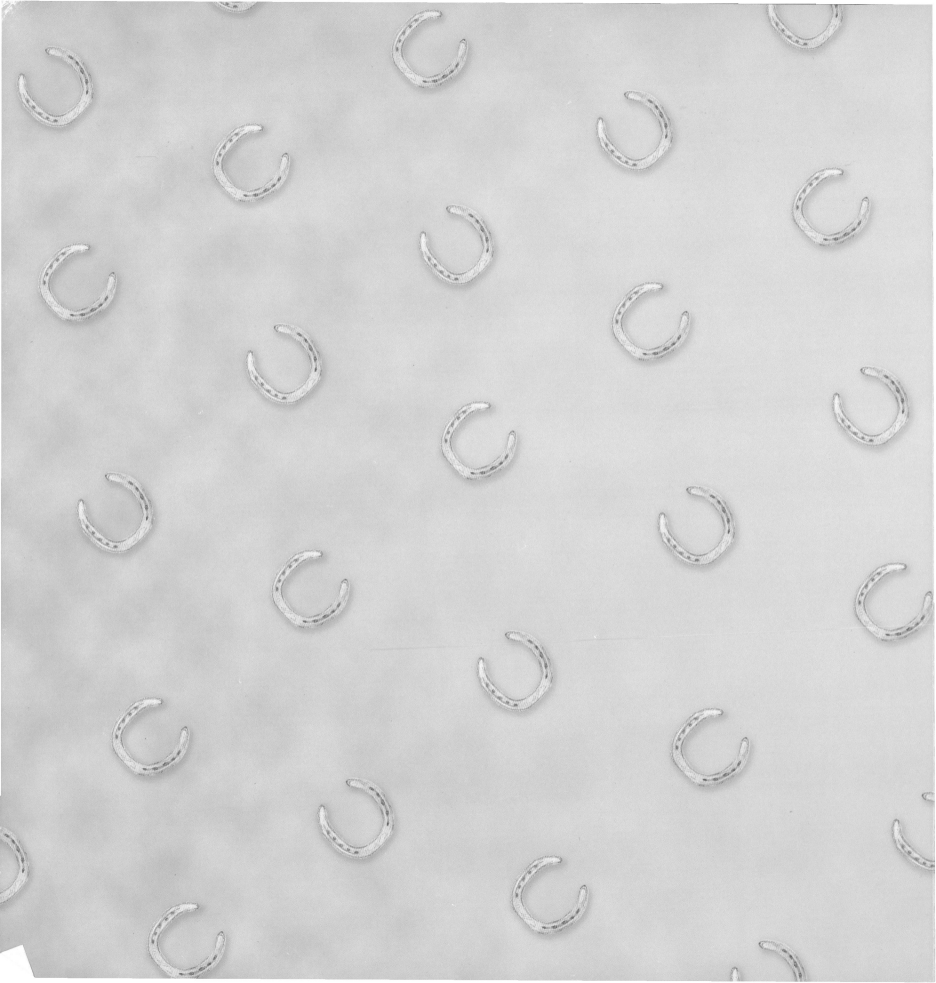